The New
EXPLORERS

New Dinosaurs

Skeletons in the Sand

Produced in cooperation with

WTTW Chicago

and

Kurtis Productions, Ltd.

Adapted by
Elaine Pascoe

 A BLACKBIRCH PRESS BOOK
WOODBRIDGE, CONNECTICUT

Published by Blackbirch Press, Inc.
260 Amity Road
Woodbridge, CT 06525

web site: http://www.blackbirch.com
email: staff@blackbirch.com

For WTTW Chicago
Edward Menaker, Executive Producer
For Kurtis Productions, Ltd.
Bill Kurtis, Executive Producer

©1998 Blackbirch Press, Inc.
First Edition

Printed in the United States of America

10 9 8 7 6 5 4 3 2 1

Library of Congress Cataloging-in-Publication Data

Pascoe, Elaine.
    New dinosaurs : skeletons in the sand / by Elaine Pascoe.
        p.   cm. — (New explorers)
    Includes bibliographical references and index.
    Summary: Follows a scientist and his team as they uncover a massive dinosaur graveyard in the Sahara Desert and discover the skeletons of two new species.
    ISBN 1-56711-231-5 (lib. bdg. : alk. paper)
    1. Dinosaurs—Sahara—Juvenile literature. 2. Sereno, Paul C.—Juvenile literature.
[1. Dinosaurs. 2. Fossils. 3. Paleontology.] I. Title. II. Series.
QE862.D5P377   1998
567.9'096626—dc21

94-43530
CIP
AC

INTRODUCTION

In 1990, I was lucky enough to help create a very special new "club." Its members come from all corners of the earth and are of all ages. They can be found braving crowded cities, floating among brilliantly colored coral reefs, and scaling desolate mountaintops. We call these people "New Explorers" because—in one way or another—they seek to uncover important knowledge or travel to places that others merely dream of.

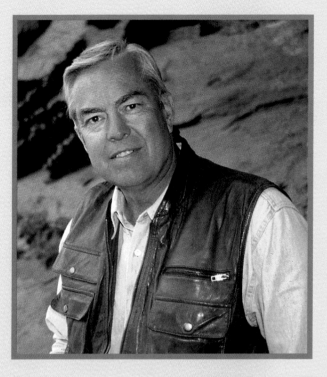

No matter where they are, or what they do, New Explorers dedicate their lives to expanding the horizons of their science. Some are biologists. Others are physicists, neurosurgeons, or ethnobotanists. Still others are engineers, teachers, even cave divers. Each of them has worked hard to push limits—to go the extra step in the pursuit of a truly significant discovery.

In his quest for a breakthrough, Mike Madden is a typical New Explorer. For eight years, he was obsessed with proving that a 27-mile (44-kilometer) underwater cave system was actually connected to the Caribbean Sea. To do this, Madden swam through tunnels never before traveled by humans. Each dive was a calculated risk—a very great one—but well worth it, for Madden also proved this was the longest underwater cave system in the world.

Madden's story, like those of all the New Explorers, is what science is all about. Science is about adventure. It's about curiosity and discovery. And, sometimes, science is also about danger.

New Explorers make it clear that science is not confined to laboratories or classrooms. They show us that science is all around us; it's at the dark and frigid bottom of our oceans, it's inside an atom, it's light-years away in a galaxy we've yet to discover. My goal—and that of this series—is to travel along with people who are pursuing the seemingly impossible, journeying into the unknown. We want to be there as scientists and innovators make their discoveries. And we want you to be part of the process of discovery as well.

Accompanying these bold and courageous individuals—and documenting their work—has not been a simple task. When Mike Madden finally made his breakthrough, I—and the New Explorers camera crew—was there in the water with him. Over the years, I have also climbed into eagles' nests, tracked a deadly virus, cut my way through thick South American rain forests, trekked deep into East Africa's Masai territory, and flown jet fighters high above the clouds with some of the U.S. Air Force's most fearless Top Guns.

As you witness the achievements we bring you through New Explorers books, you may start thinking that most of the world's great discoveries have already been made, that all the great frontiers have already been explored. But nothing could be further from the truth. In fact, scientists and researchers are now uncovering more uncharted frontiers than ever before.

As host and executive producer of our television program, my mission is to find the most fascinating and exciting New Explorers of our time. I hope that their adventures will inspire you to undertake adventures of your own—to seek out and be curious, to find answers and contemplate or create solutions. At the very best, these stories will turn you into one of the world's Newest Explorers—the men and women who will capture our imaginations and thrill us with discoveries well into the 21st century.

Bill Kurtis

Africa

At the southern end of the Sahara Desert, in the African country of Niger, scientists discover a magnificent field of dinosaur bones. There is time for only a quick look, but it is clear that the find is a scientific gold mine.

Hello, I'm Bill Kurtis. This is a brand-new species of dinosaur, discovered in 1993 in the Sahara Desert, where it had been buried for more than 100 million years. It has been named Afrovenator—or "African hunter."

These days, mounted dinosaur skeletons can be found in almost any natural history museum in the world. They are so familiar that it's easy to lose sight of what it takes to bring home an animal like this—especially today. Most of the easily reached dinosaur beds, or groups of buried bones, have already been picked clean.

In this NEW EXPLORERS journey, we will follow the pursuit of Afrovenator by a group of young people determined to succeed at something incredibly difficult.

Paul Sereno

SETTING OUT

It was 1990 when the British Museum expedition first discovered the exciting field of dinosaur bones in the Sahara. Among the members of that expedition was a young American paleontologist named Paul Sereno. He hurriedly examined the bones, and recognized their importance—skeleton upon skeleton, from one of the least-explored places and times in the history of life on Earth. He made up his mind to come back.

Now it's September 1993—three years since Paul Sereno first laid eyes on the field of dinosaur bones. For three years, he has been preparing for a tremendous expedition. His plan is to cross the world's largest desert and pull off one of the greatest dinosaur excavations in decades.

This is not the first expedition Sereno has led, but it is the biggest. He is a professor at the University of Chicago. In 1991, in Argentina, he led a team that discovered the world's most primitive dinosaur. With this trip, he hopes to discover an unknown chapter of dinosaur life in Africa.

Sereno has assembled an international team of scientists and students who will meet him in Africa in one month. But for the drive across the desert, he has chosen a young crew. They are enthusiastic—but inexperienced. Jeff Wilson is 23, a beginning graduate student at the University of Chicago. Gabrielle Lyons is 21, an undergraduate history major. Hans Larsson is also an undergraduate, from Canada. J.P. Cavigelli is from the University of Wyoming. All have been preparing for this day for a very long time.

Pangea, Triassic Period
(225 million years ago)

Jurassic-Cretaceous Period
(180 million years ago)

Late Cretaceous
(65 million years ago)

Present Day

The New
EXPLORERS

SHIFTING CONTINENTS

There are few places in Africa where rocks and dinosaur skeletons from the Cretaceous period—130 million years ago—are exposed. Sereno's young crew, however, is headed for one of the best sites in Africa. The rocks under parts of the Sahara are among the oldest in the world. Some 225 million years ago, during the Triassic period, this was the center of a supercontinent called Pangea. It was at this time that the first dinosaurs appeared. Pangea included all the world's land area, and dinosaurs and other animals roamed freely over its entire surface.

The Triassic period was followed by the Jurassic period. During the Jurassic, Pangea broke up into separate continents, which began to drift apart. It was not until 130 million years ago, during the Cretaceous period, that the continents actually broke free of each other. Then the animals on each continent became isolated. This isolation caused them to evolve differently. So far, nearly complete dinosaur skeletons from this time have been found on almost every continent except Africa. And that is why Paul Sereno and his team are headed across the Sahara—to find the dinosaurs no one else has found.

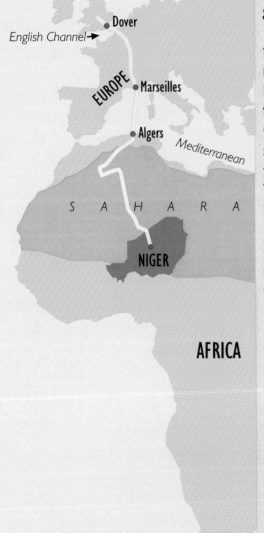

Sereno says, "We know there are going to be many, many problems and many dangers that we can't even conceive—far too numerous to count. That's the story of the expedition. We're ready for it, and we're ready to go. We've been waiting."

They leave from just outside London on the morning of a late summer day. They will not return until just before Christmas. At Dover, on the English coast, they board a ferry for France. Once across the English Channel, their route will take them straight south through France to Marseilles. There, they will cross the Mediterranean to Algiers. Then they will drive through Algeria, crossing 2,500 miles of the Sahara into Niger.

The goal of this trip is to bring back a dinosaur. But for the young people, it is an adventure that will be forever imprinted on their lives. Says Sereno, "It's got all the elements of romance, adventure, and scientific exploration in such a wonderful combination. You just describe this to anybody, and they want to come along."

At this point, Sereno and his crew are confident and assured. They have worked so hard to get ready for this trip that it's difficult to believe anything could go wrong. What they don't know is that in the coming months, they will be tested as never before—physically, intellectually, and emotionally. The experience will be much more than they imagined.

ACROSS THE DESERT

Now the true adventure begins. Once they arrive in Africa, the team passes quickly through Algiers. They cross over the Atlas Mountains into what is known as the toughest terrain on Earth: the Sahara Desert, which covers an area as large as the United States. Sereno and his crew leave behind all that is familiar. For the next month they will be camping out along the route through the desert. They will be in a very foreign land, completely out of touch with people back home.

Sereno and his crew traveled across the Sahara for a month before reaching their destination.

"This is the most dangerous part of the trip," Sereno says. "This is the part where you put your life, your future, the expedition on the line. You cannot predict who is out there, who knows you're coming, and who might stop you. It does give one the real sense of adventure, the sense that when you do succeed—and we will succeed—you've met the challenge."

The expedition was completely out of touch with the world as it traveled.

The desert landscape is part of the challenge. They pass through huge stretches of sand dunes called *ergs*, which are seas of sand. This is an environment unlike anything they've ever seen before. Jeff Wilson says: "On the whole ride down, there was a sense of awe. We would drive in some cases for hundreds and hundreds of kilometers and not see a single person, a tree, even a hill." By the third or fourth day, some of the crew begin to wonder what they have gotten themselves into.

Eventually the caravan reaches the end of the paved road. Now they follow what is called the *piste*—a road of tire tracks in the sand that leads into Niger. "You have to try to keep your speed the whole way, or you get bogged down in the sand," says Jeff. "For the whole time, it's a fight against getting stuck in the soft sand. It's really great—I love it."

Desert sand isn't the only danger. Of all the risks Sereno has taken in making this journey, one of the biggest has been leaving the United States before the government of Niger granted his expedition their final approval. Normally, permission for a project like this is merely a formality. But Sereno is headed toward a troubled region. The state department has warned that travel in the area is particularly dangerous.

"The major concern is that times have been rough on Niger, and so bandits are a problem," says Paul. "We're moving into the area with a whole set of vehicles and all sorts of equipment that is difficult to buy, and therefore quite valuable."

"This is the part where you put your life, your future, the expedition on the line."

For centuries, the northern part of Niger has been home to a group of nomadic people called Tauregs, who struggle to maintain an ancient culture and customs. They were once warriors who controlled the trade route across the Sahara. Today, they make up just 10 percent of the population of Niger, and increasingly they find themselves as outcasts.

Several years before Sereno set out, the Tauregs joined in an armed rebellion, seeking independence. Now a truce has been declared, but the region is still unstable. Reports of banditry continue. Most westerners stay out of northern Niger.

Despite their worries, the expedition members find themselves clearly welcomed when, after 20 days, the team reaches Agadez, a city in central Niger, close to the field of dinosaur bones. Most of the team will stay there while Sereno and a few others head south to Niamey, Niger's capital, to check in with government authorities about their official clearance.

The Sahara has been home to the nomadic Tuaregs for centuries.

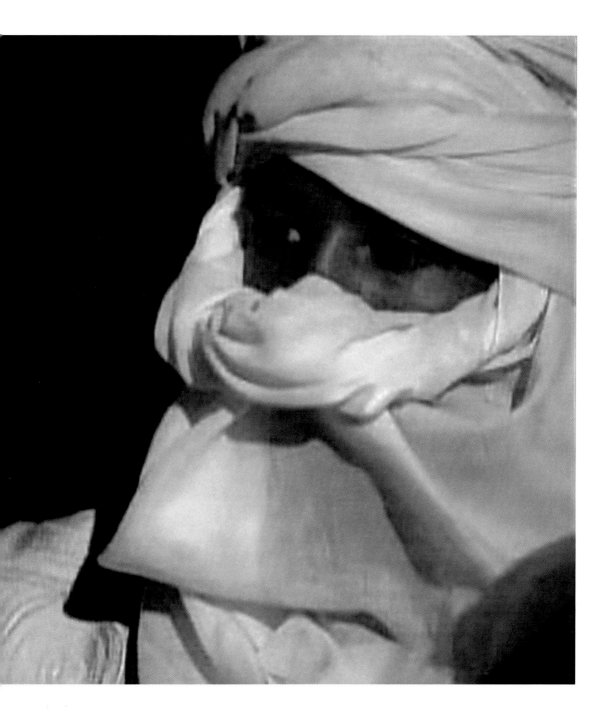

To paleontologist Paul Sereno, Africa represents the greatest frontier for research into the age of dinosaurs. That's because so little is known about the dinosaurs that once lived there. "Almost anything you pull out of the ground is going to be new, and will shed light on major groups of dinosaurs for the whole continent," he says. "That's basically why I came and assembled the group.

"I've been to many other continents looking for dinosaur fossils, and this portion of Africa really outstrips any other experience. It's just awe-inspiring. There's nowhere else where discoveries can contribute so heavily to what we know about an entire time period."

A Tangle of Paperwork and Waiting

It's a 600-mile trip from Agadez to Niamey, but it's like traveling from one world to another—leaving the desert and entering the hot, humid climate of Africa south of the Sahara. In Niamey, Sereno learns that permission for the expedition has not been granted. Furthermore, the U.S. embassy will not help, insisting that the area in the north is simply too dangerous.

Sereno is determined to press on. He begins a massive campaign of letters and phone calls, designed to convince a series of government officials to give the expedition a chance. His partner in the negotiations is Didier Dutheil, a Frenchman who joined the expedition in Paris. In all, they will need approval to be granted from four separate ministries. The process is especially difficult because Niger just recently had its first democratic elections. The government Sereno is trying to work with is brand new.

The city of Agadez in Niger

In Niamey, Sereno waited for official approval for weeks.

> "It's basically the biggest bureaucratic nightmare you could possibly imagine."

The team, waiting in Agadez, is optimistic. Catherine Foster, a paleontologist from the University of Chicago, explains: "This is just the way things operate. Permission will come, and when it does we're going to be really ready to get out of here and set up camp."

Sereno is also optimistic. It seems the permission is just within their grasp. With promises of imminent approval, he gives a green light for the rest of the team to fly into Niger. A dozen scientists arrive and head up to Agadez to join the others. As they move farther north, the presence of the military increases—suggesting that the U.S. embassy's concerns about security may be very real.

But back in Niamey, Sereno's push for approval is taking much longer than he expected. While his request is shuffled from one government ministry to another, the days of waiting turn into weeks of waiting. The team members in Agadez try to make the most of an increasingly bad situation. They set out to see for themselves if the area is dangerous. And the reports they hear are not good. It becomes clear that, if they do work, the protection of an armed guard will be necessary.

With that in mind, team members begin to question whether the pursuit of their science is worth the risk of personal harm. Says Catherine Foster, "Had we known this was the situation before we came here, I don't think we would have come. Now what do we do? Is it worth going on with this? Is it safe enough to go on? Or should we say, 'Look, this is too much. Let's stop this now and re-evaluate the whole thing.'"

Paleontologist Catherine Foster

The lines of the debate are drawn as older, more experienced expedition members argue that the area is too dangerous, while young students continue to hold out hope. Sereno's team begins to fall apart. Some people—mainly those with field experience—decide to leave. Making matters worse, the expedition is quickly running out of money. Funds that were scheduled to be flown in have been held up by an airline strike.

The pressure on Sereno is tremendous. He sees his dream coming to an end. His three years of work, the opportunity to make a significant scientific discovery—all of it is slipping away. It is difficult to remember the confidence of departure day in London almost two months earlier. With so many obstacles in the way, and no solution in sight, Sereno goes to Agadez and calls the expedition off.

"It's basically the biggest bureaucratic nightmare you could possibly imagine," Sereno says. But miraculously, within the next 48 hours everything falls into place. Final and full permission is granted for the project. Necessary money is flown in. And Sereno determines that what seemed impossible two days ago is suddenly possible once again.

The expedition can go forward—but not without a price. Many in the group decide that the risks are too great for what can be accomplished in the time that is left. Ten members decide to go home, and ten decide to stay. Most of those who stay made the drive across the desert. Some are young students with absolutely no experience.

After more than a month of waiting, the team headed to the first site.

THE FOSSIL FIELD

A full two months after they left London, and more than a month after they arrived in Niger, the remaining expedition members are finally ready to dig up dinosaurs. They have come to a small oasis town close to the field of fossils. There, Sereno has rented a compound where they can stay. "We waited in Niger almost 40 days—40 days and 40 nights—and it's paying off," he says. "We're about to head out. Everyone's up."

Now all they have to do is find the bones that Sereno found three years earlier. He calls the site Fako, after the name of the ancient riverbed in which it is located. Fragments of dinosaur bones were first discovered here in the 1940s by French scientists, but since then the area has been largely overlooked.

When they reach the site, they find at long last, what they came so far to see. For Paul Sereno, it is a powerful moment. The area is so rich in fossils that team members must be careful where they walk, to avoid damaging skeletons. Sereno's guess is that as many as eight dinosaurs may have been buried here more than 130 million years ago. Over time, the soft ground surrounding the harder fossilized bone has been eroded—worn away by wind and water—leaving the animals exposed for discovery.

Members of the team set to work quickly at the Fako site.

Fako was unexpectedly rich in fossils.

The decision on how to proceed is critical. The team has just 28 days to spend in the field, and no one wants to come out empty-handed. Sereno picks a place to start the digging. The goal is to unearth complete skeletons of new dinosaurs, so team members begin searching for bones that are articulated, or connected. Connected bones may indicate that there is more beneath the ground.

The New EXPLORERS

FOSSILS: MESSAGES FROM THE PAST

The last dinosaurs died out 65 million years ago, millions of years before the first humans walked the earth. Everything we know about these amazing animals has been learned by studying fossils— remains of ancient life that have been preserved in the ground. Fossils form only in special conditions. Here's how some of the fossils found by Paul Sereno and his team may have formed:

Perhaps 120 million years ago, a dinosaur died, and its body washed into a stream. The soft parts of its body decayed quickly, leaving only hard parts, such as bones and teeth. Layers of sand and mud soon covered these hard body parts. Over many years, the original bone material was replaced by minerals that seeped through the mud. Gradually, what were once bones became bone-shaped rocks—fossils. Millions of years went by. The stream dried up, and the land changed. Wind and water then eroded the softer rock around the fossilized bones, exposing them to view.

Some expedition members are skilled at reading the land for indications of fossils below. "You never know what's underneath," says Bill Simpson of the Field Museum in Chicago. "You have to go by surface indications." The first day is disappointing—small fragments of bone, bits and pieces too damaged to be useful. But on the second day, they get the break they need.

The articulated bones of a large sauropod were waiting for the expedition at Fako.

Top: Sauropod bones as they lay in the ground.
Above: The bones as they fit into the sauropod's body.

The New
EXPLORERS

GIANT PLANT EATERS

The first new dinosaur that Paul Sereno and his team uncover near Fako belongs to a group called sauropods. The animals in this group are all plant eaters, with long necks, stout bodies, and long tails. They include dinosaurs like Diplodocus and other giants of the dinosaur era, animals that may have weighed 40 tons (36,288 kilograms) or more. In comparison, an African elephant, the largest land mammal of today, weighs about 5 tons (4,536 kilograms). The dinosaur from Fako is most similar to Camarasaurus, a dinosaur found in North America. That surprises the researchers because in North America, Camarasaurus died out 30 million years before the African dinosaur lived. They wonder: Did some kinds of dinosaurs live on in Africa for millions of years after those like them disappeared from other parts of the world?

Sereno and a few others go out exploring. Just a short distance from Fako, they find a beautifully preserved upper arm of an enormous dinosaur, along with bones from the animal's hand. The bones are articulated, and they seem to lead into the ground. The question is: How much more of this animal is buried here?

The enthusiastic team sets to work. As they excavate the forearm, a hind limb is discovered. More bones from the hand are found. The next day, they find a section of the backbone. Soon it is clear that much of the animal is under the ground. Ribs, a pelvic (hip) bone, and more vertebrae emerge. Simpson says, "We have exposed 10 or 11 bones, mostly articulated. It doesn't get any better than that."

Uncovering the bones safely is a slow and painstaking job.

Paul Sereno works on exposing parts of the sauropod skeleton.

Paleontologist Bill Simpson works at the Field Museum in Chicago. For him, the expedition to Africa is a new experience. "There is a certain romance to being the first to do research in an area. I've tried to imagine what that's like, and now I'm getting an idea because we're among the first paleontologists to arrive in this part of Africa, to excavate and do research here. And it's thrilling to be one of the first ones."

Most exciting of all is the fact that the animal they are uncovering is a completely new species of dinosaur. The days of work should be exhausting, but no one is tired. On the long ride back to the compound, there is a wonderful sense of anticipation of what the next day will bring. They thought they would be at this site for three days, but as the days wear on, the discoveries keep coming. "We are seeing stuff that few if any people have ever seen before," says team member J.P. Cavigelli. "Everything is brand new here."

With everyone working hard and concentrating on the site, the much-talked-about security problems are forgotten. Still, after a few days, the local police arrange for an armed escort to follow the crew. Before long, the escort, too, is forgotten. The team establishes a grueling routine of incredibly long days.

While some members of the expedition continue to collect the bones, others work to understand how this animal came to be here. They dig a trench to get a look at a geologic section—a cross-section of earth that will show how the environment changed over time. They also map the placement of the bones in the ground. This will help them understand how the animal died, and how it was moved after death. They find that the dinosaur died on its right side, was washed into a stream, and was buried almost immediately, perhaps in a few hours.

A huge humerus (arm bone) was uncovered at Fako.

"Everything
is brand
new here."

Paleontologists measure the various layers of rock
at a site to find clues to its geologic history.

The crew prepares the ancient bones for the long trip home. Without protection, the fossils will crumble into powder when they are loaded onto trucks and carried out of the desert. Expedition members cover each bone with a layer of paper or aluminum and then wrap it in plaster bandages. When the bandages dry, the brittle fossil is protected by a sort of plaster cast. Prepared for travel, some of the huge bones weigh hundreds of pounds.

Meanwhile, with time running out, team members step up their search to learn what else may be hidden in these rocks. They begin their prospecting at sunrise—and it seems there are bones everywhere they look.

Members of the expedition spent long, tireless days digging in the Sahara.

A Major Find

With a shout, Hans Larsson calls other team members to see what he has found. "This is a footprint of a theropod, a carnivorous dinosaur. It walked on two legs," he says. "It looked like a chicken when it walked. This footprint actually preserves an animal walking on wet sand 120 million years ago—that's fantastic."

The footprint that Hans Larsson found belongs to one of the dinosaurs that preyed on the huge sauropod the team found earlier. The question looms large: Can they find the predator's bones? There is almost no record of what flesh-eating dinosaurs looked like in Africa during this period. To find one would be a major discovery—and, incredibly, they succeed. It's the kind of find that will earn this expedition a place in the history of dinosaur exploration.

Paul Sereno and Jeff Wilson examine the way in which the bones of a dinosaur lie in the fossil field.

THE AFRICAN HUNTER

The flesh-eating dinosaur discovered by the African expedition belongs to a group of dinosaurs called theropods. All the dinosaurs in this group are meat eaters, with powerful hind legs, sharp claws for grasping prey, sharp teeth, and powerful jaws. The most famous dinosaur in this group is Tyrannosaurus rex, a fearsome North American predator that was one of the last and largest meat eaters.

Sereno named the new theropod Afrovenator—"African hunter." When the bones he found were prepared at the Royal Ontario Museum in Toronto, Canada, the world got its first good look at a predatory dinosaur that evolved on the isolated continent of Africa. The African dinosaur was 20 to 25 feet (7.6 meters) long. Like other theropods, it ran on two legs and probably used its hands to catch prey. Its feet had three well-developed toes pointing forward, with the middle toes the longest—like the feet of modern birds. Afrovenator was a distant cousin of Tyrannosaurus. Sereno concluded that the two dinosaurs must have shared a common ancestor, not yet discovered, that lived before the supercontinent Pangea broke apart.

Sereno believes Tyrannosaurus Rex was a distant cousin of Afrovenator.

By the time they have spent eight days at the site, the team has found enough to begin to construct a very clear picture of this enormous animal. "It's complete, and it's absolutely bizarre," says Sereno. There's a tremendous sense of relief. From the beginning of the expedition, there was no guarantee that they would actually contribute something to science. Now they know that they will go home with something no one has ever seen before.

DINOSAUR TIMELINE: THE MESOZOIC ERA

Dinosaurs roamed the earth for about 160 million years, in an era called the Mesozoic. This era, which began about 248 million years ago, is now commonly divided into three periods, called the Triassic, the Jurassic, and the Cretaceous. Below is a basic timeline of the Mesozoic era, when the earth's largest and most powerful creatures ruled the planet.

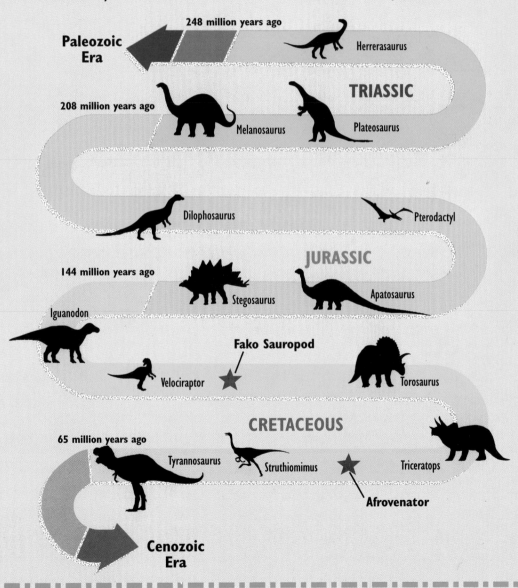

248 million years ago

Paleozoic Era

Herrerasaurus

TRIASSIC

208 million years ago

Melanosaurus

Plateosaurus

Dilophosaurus

Pterodactyl

JURASSIC

144 million years ago

Stegosaurus

Apatosaurus

Iguanodon

Fako Sauropod

Velociraptor

Torosaurus

CRETACEOUS

65 million years ago

Tyrannosaurus

Struthiomimus

Afrovenator

Triceratops

Cenozoic Era

Below right and left: Work was completed at Fako while the theropod was being uncovered at another site.

With only 14 days left, there is no time to rest. They begin to tackle the fossils of the flesh-eating dinosaur. The collecting style is different from the one they used to dig up the huge sauropod bones at the Fako site. These bones are smaller and more delicate. They lie just below the surface and can fall apart easily.

Sereno says, "The big sauropod skeleton certainly would have lasted several more years, parts of it hundreds of years. But this skeleton would have been washed away in a few years because the bones are so close to the surface." Some of the most delicate fossils are the skull bones. They are also the most important for understanding exactly what type of animal this was. In this case, the dinosaur's skull is huge—at least 2 feet (.6 meter) long.

Uncovering fossils that are millions of years old requires great care and patience.

Jeff Wilson is one of the youngest and least experienced team members. For him, the trip is an important personal experience.

"Every day on the site, we were doing all sorts of stuff we didn't know how to do before," Jeff says. "Paul wanted this to be the greatest trip of everybody's life. I think it has been."

> **"There was a tremendous feeling that we had accomplished what people said we couldn't"**

"The trip was not just about dinosaurs. It may sound kind of cheesy, but the trip was about making a dream come true, being dedicated to an idea, and being willing to stick something out and really see it happen."

Another young team member adds, "Getting a taste of what it's like to be a paleontologist, the flavor of what it's like to be in the field—that sort of turned on a switch inside me I didn't know was there. And there was a tremendous feeling that we had accomplished what people said we couldn't do, that we had come out with something that was going to last and that was really important."

By the second day, Sereno and his crew know they have a fairly complete skeleton. They have parts of both hind limbs, much of the hand and forearm, the shoulder blade, and vertebrae from several areas. That gives them a picture of the animal: A two-legged predator that probably chased live prey, caught it in its hands, and ripped off large pieces of flesh with its monstrous jaws. It's a truly thrilling discovery—in two days, they've found more of a predatory African dinosaur than had been found over the last century.

The bones of Afrovenator as they lay in the sand. The bone section on the right once contained the eye socket.

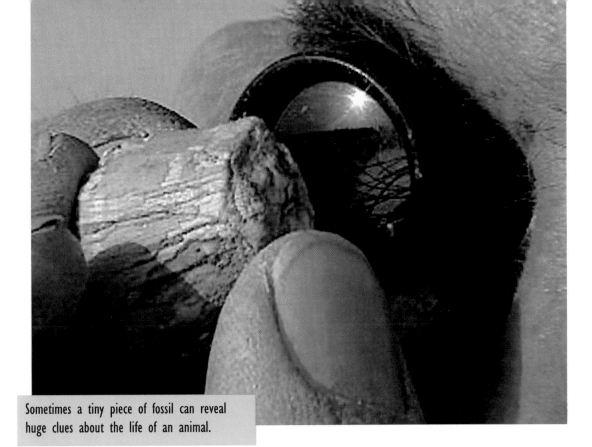

Sometimes a tiny piece of fossil can reveal huge clues about the life of an animal.

HEADING HOME

After nearly a month, the work in the field is finally finished. The team members have accomplished all that they can. In an amazingly short time, however, they have found and excavated two new species of dinosaurs. And with their discoveries, they have begun to fill in one of the last missing chapters in the story of dinosaur evolution.

Paul Sereno, Hans Larsson, and Jeff Wilson study the position of a large leg bone.

Pieces of the theropod skeleton are placed in position.

The team hurries to pack up for the trip home. They have reservations on a ferry leaving Algiers on December 15. If they miss that boat, they could be stuck in Africa for weeks. Among the last-minute details: Loading 6 tons (5,443 kilograms) of dinosaur bones into the back of a truck. With much groaning and shouting, the job is done. The team is ready to go.

Below: The bones are carefully wrapped in plaster bandages before they are transported.

Once the plaster is dry, the bones can be rolled into position.

With some help from local people, the expedition loaded about 6 tons (5,433 kilograms) of bones.

"The only thing that was on our minds when we were leaving was when we would have a chance to come back. In all of our hearts was the desire to someday return," says Sereno. Yet going home is also a triumph. The mission has been accomplished, and the proof is in the back of the truck. And after two months camping out in the desert, team members find that walking into a hotel in Algiers is like walking into another world. From here on, it's pure celebration.

The expedition headed home with more than they ever dreamed possible.

"Somehow you overcome what you have to overcome," Sereno says.

Sereno credits the team for the expedition's success. "These are people who can do it all," he says. A field expedition, he adds, is "like the decathlon of science: You have to be able to survive a desert, not only immerse yourself in other cultures but actually enjoy it. So these are some very special people." They were also determined to succeed. "You set out to do something with the mind and heart to do it, and it's going to happen one way or the other. There are risks enough to take the nerves out of anybody at one time or another, and this trip certainly has had that. Somehow you overcome what you have to overcome."

In many ways, this story has just begun. Sereno and his team opened a frontier, and others will certainly follow. As for Afrovenator, the skeletal cast will go back to Niger—the country that ultimately opened its doors to the team and the special place that still holds so much to be discovered.

Paul Sereno's quest in the Sahara opened the door to unlimited new discoveries in the future.

GLOSSARY

articulated Connected at a joint.

eroded Worn away.

evolve Gradually develop.

fossils Hardened remains of ancient animals or plants.

geologic section A cross section of earth that shows the different layers put down over time.

paleontologist A scientist who studies prehistoric life, mainly through fossils.

predator An animal that kills and eats other animals.

sauropod One of a group of plant-eating dinosaurs with long necks, stout bodies, and long tails.

theropod One of a group of meat-eating dinosaurs with powerful hind legs, sharp teeth and claws, and powerful jaws.

vertebrae Bones that form the spine.

FURTHER READING

Dingus, Lowell. *What Color Is That Dinosaur?* Brookfield, CT: Millbrook Press, 1994.

Farlow, James O., and Ralph E. Molnar. *The Great Hunters: Meat-Eating Dinosaurs and Their World.* New York: Franklin Watts, 1995.

Farlow, James O. *On the Tracks of Dinosaurs: A Study of Dinosaur Footprints.* New York: Franklin Watts, 1991.

Horner, Jack, and Don Lessem. *Digging Up Tyrannosaurus Rex.* New York: Random House, 1992.

Lasky, Kathryn. *Dinosaur Dig.* New York: Morrow, 1990.

Norell, Mark. *All You Need to Know About Dinosaurs.* New York: Sterling, 1990.

Weishampel, David B. *Plant-Eating Dinosaurs.* New York: Franklin Watts, 1992.

Web Sites

http://www.pbs.org/wttw/web_newexp/
The official homepage of The New Explorers television series. Lists the show broadcast schedule, educational resources, and information about how to join The New Explorers Club as well as how to participate in The New Explorers electronic field trip.

http://www.dinosociety.org/
The Dinosaur Society—Learn about recent dinosaur discoveries, visit a dig, join the Dinosaur Society Penpal Network.

http://www.bvis.uic.edu/museum/Home.html
Take a virtual tour through the Field Museum of Natural History's exhibits. Features animations, interactive games, and educational resources.

http://www.ucmp.berkeley.edu/fosrec/fosrec.html
Learning from the fossil record—a collection of educational resources and classroom activities.

http://www.txdirect.net/users/jmayer/fon.html
Focus on Niger: Information and photographs as well as other African-related links.

http://www.englib.cornell.edu/pri/pri1.html
The Paleontological Research Institution—take a "virtual field trip," browse through an enormous fossil collection, discover resources to utilize in the classroom.

Index

Photo Credits

Page 3: Bill Arnold
Pages 23, 25: Will Crockett
All other photographic images: © Kurtis Productions Ltd. and WTTW/Chicago
Maps and charts: © Blackbirch Press, Inc.